WILDLIFE AT RISK

ENDANGERED
GORILLAS

Jane Katirgis and Carl R. Green

Enslow Publishing
101 W. 23rd Street
Suite 240
New York, NY 10011
USA

enslow.com

Published in 2016 by Enslow Publishing, LLC.
101 W. 23rd Street, Suite 240, New York, NY 10011

Library of Congress Cataloging-in-Publication Data

Katirgis, Jane, author.
 Endangered gorillas / Jane Katirgis and Carl R. Green.
    pages cm. — (Wildlife at risk)
 Summary: "Discusses gorillas, why they are endangered, and how they are being helped"—Provided by publisher.
 Audience: Ages 11+.
 Audience: Grades 7 to 8.
 Includes bibliographical references and index.
 ISBN 978-0-7660-6898-8 (library binding)
 ISBN 978-0-7660-6896-4 (pbk.)
 ISBN 978-0-7660-6897-1 (6-pack)
 1. Gorilla—Juvenile literature. 2. Endangered species—Juvenile literature. 3. Gorilla—Conservation—Juvenile literature. I. Green, Carl R., author. II. Title.
 QL737.P94K37 2016
 599.884—dc23
                           2015009976

Printed in the United States of America

To Our Readers: We have done our best to make sure all Web site addresses in this book were active and appropriate when we went to press. However, the author and the publisher have no control over and assume no liability for the material available on those Web sites or on any Web sites they may link to. Any comments or suggestions can be sent by e-mail to customerservice@enslow.com.

Portions of this book originally appeared in the book *The Gorilla*.

Photos Credits: Ariadne Van Zandbergen/Lonely Planet Images/Getty Images, p. 1 (gorillas); Creativ Studio Heinemann/Creative (RF)/Getty Images, p. 1 (borage flowers); FRANK RUMPENHORST/AFP/Getty Images, p. 37; hudiemm/E+/Getty Images (notebook fact boxes throughout book); iPics/Shutterstock.com, p. 24; Joakim Leroy/E+/Getty Images, p. 1 (palm leaf); John Warden/Photolibrary/Getty Images, p. 17; © Keystone Pictures USA/ZUMAPRESS.com, p. 9; Last Refuge/Robert Harding World Imagery/Getty Images, p. 33; Maria Toutoudaki/Photodisk/Getty Images (background paper texture throughout book); Martyn Colbeck/Oxford Scientific/Gety Images, p. 23; Mint Images - Art Wolfe/Mint Images RF/Getty Images, p. 10; Neil Selkirk/The LIFE Images Collection/Getty Images, p. 29; Nigel Pavitt/AWL Images/Getty Images, p. 35; Per-Anders Pettersson/The image Bank/Getty Images, p. 22; Peter Stuckings/Lonely Planet Images/Getty images, p. 39; Robert J. Ross/Photolibrary/Getty Images, p. 31; STEPHANIE AGLIETTI/AFP/Getty Images, p. 41; Thomas Marent/Visuals Unlimited, Inc/Getty Images, p. 15; Wolfgang Kaehler/LightRocket via Getty Images, p. 32.

Cover Credits: Ariadne Van Zandbergen/Lonely Planet Images/Getty Images (gorillas); Creativ Studio Heinemann/Creative (RF)/Getty Images (borage flowers); Joakim Leroy/E+/Getty Images (palm leaf); Maria Toutoudaki/Photodisk/Getty Images (background paper texture).

CONTENTS

GORILLAS AT A GLANCE

Scientific Name

Gorilla gorilla. The species divides into three subspecies: western lowland gorilla *(Gorilla gorilla gorilla),* eastern lowland gorilla *(Gorilla gorilla graueri),* and mountain gorilla *(Gorilla gorilla beringei).*

Closest Relatives

Chimpanzees, bonobos (pygmy chimpanzees), orangutans, and humans.

Current Habitat

Western lowland gorillas are found in west-central Africa. Eastern lowland gorillas live in the eastern part of the Congo. Mountain gorillas roam the Virunga Volcanoes region of east-central Africa.

Size and Weight*

Mountain Gorilla:
Adult Male: Height: 5 ft., 8 in. (1.7 m)
   Arm Span: 7 ft., 6 in. (2.3 m)
   Weight: 350 lbs. (159 kg)
Adult Female: Height: 5 ft. (1.5 m)
   Arm Span: 6 ft., 4 in. (1.9 m)
   Weight: 190 lbs. (86 kg)

Diet

Gorillas feed on up to 220 plant species and favor the leaves, shoots, fruit, and stems. A large male can eat 40 pounds (18 kg) of food in a day.

Current Populations

Western lowland gorillas—about 100,000
Eastern lowland gorillas—fewer than 3,000
Mountain Gorillas—about 880

Special Adaptations

Gorillas, along with chimpanzees and orangutans, display a capacity for complex learning. Some captive gorillas have been taught to communicate with humans by using sign language.

Life Span

In the wild: about 30 years.
In captivity: 35 years or longer. As many as four out of ten wild gorillas die before their sixth birthday.

Vocalizations

Gorillas produce more than twenty different sounds when excited. The sounds range from soft purrs and grunts to loud screeches and roars.

Main Threats

Loss of habitat, poaching, and exposure to diseases.

Legislative Status

All gorillas, particularly the mountain gorilla, are included on endangered species lists. The Great Apes Conservation Act, passed by the US Congress in 2000, commits the United States to the struggle to save *Gorilla gorilla*.

Organizations Working to Save the Gorilla

Dian Fossey Gorilla Fund

International Gorilla Conservation Progamme (IGCP)

Wildlife Conservation Society

World Wildlife Fund

*Figures represent average measurements.

chapter one
MEET *GORILLA GORILLA*

Have you ever visited a zoo and spent time admiring the gorillas? Perhaps you were delighted by the playful youngsters chasing each other. Or maybe you were intrigued by the thoughtful looks of adults as they stared back at you. It is not surprising that these primates seem so familiar to us. Up to 99 percent of their DNA is the same as human DNA. However, myths in the past have painted a more aggressive picture of these primates.

For the past four hundred years, reports out of Africa painted the gorilla, to quote 1800s explorer Paul du Chaillu, as a "hellish dream creature, . . . half man, half beast."[1] Another work tells us that pregnant Bantu and pygmy women believed that silverback gorillas would attack them and kill their babies.[2]

Hollywood added to the myth in the classic 1933 film *King Kong*. This is the plot: While shooting on a remote island, filmmakers run into a 30-foot (9-m) gorilla known as King Kong. As the cameras roll, the snarling, chest-thumping Kong storms into a native village. In the panic that follows, Kong grabs young Ann Darrow (played by Fay Wray) and carries her away. Instead of killing her, the great ape falls in love with his prize. Undaunted, the film crew rescues Ann, captures Kong, and takes him back to New York. There, Kong escapes, seizes Ann, and climbs the Empire State Building. The police are forced to call in Navy warplanes. A baffled Kong swats at the planes until machine-gun fire sends him crashing to the pavement far below.[3]

A Better Understanding

The ferocious gorilla myth survived until modern naturalists rewrote it. George Schaller, first on the scene, began his landmark studies in 1959. He ventured into the jungle unarmed despite old stories of gorillas that crushed rifles with their teeth. "No animal attacks without good cause," Schaller reasoned. "My inclination is to give the charging animal the benefit of the doubt, hoping that it is merely bluffing." The insight turned out to be correct. Schaller lived among gorillas for two years, and never once did a gorilla seriously threaten him.[4]

Schaller detailed his findings in *The Mountain Gorilla* (1963) and *The Year of the Gorilla* (1964). Some of his conclusions laid the old myths to rest. First, he found that gorillas are shy, peaceful plant eaters. The scary chest-beating displays the males put on are meant to frighten intruders. If the visitor does not make any threatening moves, the gorillas relax and back away. Dian Fossey, who picked up where Schaller left off, reported similar findings in her book, *Gorillas in the Mist* (1983). Once she began acting like one of the group, the gorillas accepted her. Fossey imitated

their feeding and grooming habits and even learned to belch like a gorilla.[5]

Schaller and Fosse further blurred the line that divides humans and apes. Gorillas, the naturalists found, use human-like gestures, postures, and expressions. When they wake up in the morning, gorillas stretch and yawn. If upset, they frown. Like any angry two-year-old child, young gorillas throw temper tantrums. Within their family groups, relations tend to be warm and caring.[6] Maybe, scientists reasoned, gorillas can learn to talk.

A Gorilla Named Koko

Photographer Mike Nichols met a new friend some years ago. "She welcomed me into her trailer," he writes, "and asked what I had in my purse. Did I have a lipstick? A mirror? Could she look at my teeth?" Most people would have thought these were strange questions. Nichols, however, felt right at home with Hanabi-Ko, Koko for short. Koko is a western lowland gorilla who talks to visitors in sign language.[7]

Psychologist Dr. Francine "Penny" Patterson adopted ten-month-old Koko in 1972. She knew that chimpanzees had learned to use American Sign Language (ASL). If chimps could do it, why not gorillas? Having been raised in a zoo, Koko was used to being around people. Over the years, Koko has learned more than a thousand signs. Follow this ASL exchange between Koko and one of her trainers, Barbara Hiller.

Koko and psychologist Penny Patterson communicate through sign language.

Hiller: What do you say when you really want to insult people?
Koko: Dirty.
Hiller: Okay, can you think of another one?
Koko: Sorry, gorilla polite.
Hiller: It's okay to tell me.
Koko: Toilet.[8]

If she is truly upset, Koko is likely to call someone a dirty, bad toilet. Her other behaviors seem equally human. When Penny scolds her, she sometimes lies to escape being given a time out.

Gorillas have humanlike gestures and expressions. This gorilla is resting its head against its hand and looks deep in thought.

And when her pet kitten was killed, she made sad hooting sounds. Then she signed, "Sleep, cat."

Whether captive or wild, gorillas are an endangered species. Of the three subspecies, the western lowland gorilla survives in the greatest numbers. About 100,000 still live in six central African countries. By contrast, some estimates say fewer than 3,000 eastern lowland gorillas roam their remote habitat in the Congo. With only about 880 survivors, mountain gorillas are even closer to extinction.

The campaign to save the gorilla has gained worldwide support. Penny Patterson's Gorilla Foundation is doing its part by carving out a sanctuary on the Hawaiian island of Maui. Koko will one day live there in a setting much like that enjoyed by her wild African cousins.

chapter two

JUNGLE GORILLA

In the middle of the day on the slope of a forest in Africa, all is quiet. The sun is bright in the sky, and blooming flowers add a pop of color to the sea of green plants. Under a tree, a dozen mountain gorillas recline in the shade. An enormous silverback is the leader of the troop, and the adults gather around him. After a morning spent eating wild plants, such as bamboo, the gorillas all appear to be happy to rest.

When it is nap time for the adults, it is playtime for the youngsters. A group of three-year-olds swing from limb to limb in the huge tree. The smallest gorilla, barely past the toddler stage, slides down the silverback's great round belly. The silverback reaches out and tickles the little one with his huge hand. A juvenile wanders off, only to be called back by his mother's warning grunt.

The hours drift past. At last, the silverback stirs and stretches. Then he lumbers to his feet and leads the group to a new feeding place.[1] Gorillas have been living by this script for millions of years.

Primates

African children like to listen to stories of how the natural world came to be. One old tale says that gorillas once were people—lazy people. Too slothful to make clothes or build houses, they let hair grow all over their bodies. Another story spins a yarn about wereapes, an African version of werewolves. Gorillas, some whisper, are human during the day. It is only at night that they turn into apes.[2]

Naturalists tell a more fact-based story. Gorillas, they say, belong to a family of mammals known as primates. Tiny at first but growing ever larger, early primates were gifted with good brains. In time they learned to depend more on their forward-facing eyes than on their sense of smell. Instead of paws, they developed hands and feet that could grasp fruit and branches. Females gave birth to babies who needed long months of care. Today, nonhuman primates roam the wilds of Africa, Asia, and the Americas. Humans, a more widespread species known as *Homo sapiens*, have even walked on the moon.[3]

The first gorillas most likely appeared in Africa about ten million years ago. The date is vague because *Gorilla gorilla* has always lived in rain forests. Bones decay quickly in the damp soil. Without fossils, naturalists cannot fully reconstruct their family tree. Studies do show that the great apes—gorillas, chimpanzees, bonobos (pygmy chimps), and orangutans—are closely related. A gorilla's DNA differs from that of a chimpanzee by only 2.3 percent. Chimps and humans differ by even less—1.6 percent.

A Look at Gorillas

Somewhere along the way, climate change scattered the species. As the groups adapted to new African habitats, three subspecies emerged. Western lowland gorillas (*Gorilla gorilla gorilla*) have broader faces and smaller jaws. The hair on their heads is reddish brown, while the rest of the body is a brownish gray. The black-haired eastern lowland gorillas (*Gorilla gorilla graueri*) are the largest of the three. Mountain gorillas (*Gorilla gorilla beringei*) are also black and weigh in somewhere between the other two. To survive the high-altitude cold, mountain gorillas grow denser, longer coats than their lowland cousins. Some scientists believe there are two separate species of gorillas with five subspecies.

Adult male and female gorillas are easy to tell apart. A full-grown male is nearly twice as large as the female. A 5-foot 8-inch (1.7-m) male mountain gorilla weighs in at around 350 pounds (159 kg). His 5-foot (1.5-m) mate will likely tip the scales at 190 pounds (86 kg). A mature male is known as a silverback, a tribute to the saddle of silver-white fur that covers his back. A silverback also develops a high crown of bone and muscle atop his head, known as the sagittal crest.

Fast Fact!

Mountain gorillas have longer hair; lowland gorillas have shorter, soft hair.

Silverback gorillas use the backs of their hands for balance as they move around.

Viewed up close, a gorilla's skin is shiny and jet black. Its eyes are widely spaced, and the small ears lay flat against the head. Folds of skin surround two large flared nostrils. Like human fingerprints, each gorilla nose print is different. Researchers use these nose prints to tell one gorilla from another. A gorilla's hand looks much like a human hand, except for having a shorter thumb. The arms are longer and more powerful and the legs much shorter. As a result, the gorilla cannot walk upright for long distances. When moving about, gorillas knuckle walk using the back of their hands for balance.[4]

A Day in the Life

Gorillas are found in rain forest habitats. Western lowland gorillas live in the low-lying swamps and forests of west-central Africa. The eastern lowland gorillas of the Congo range through bamboo forests that climb to 7,800 feet (2,377 m). High in the Virunga Volcanoes, mountain gorillas bed down at the 13,000-foot (3,962- m) level. Each subspecies feeds on a mix of plant foods native to its habitat. A mountain gorilla's diet is 85 percent leaves, shoots, and stems. Grubs, snails, ants, and termites make up only 0.1 percent of its food intake. The western lowland gorilla's warmer habitat provides the fruit that supplies 67 percent of its diet. Termites and insect larvae add another 3 percent.[5]

A gorilla's life centers on its family group. A normal group is made up of a dominant silverback, two or three younger males, and several adult females and their offspring. The group travels, feeds, plays, and sleeps together. Western lowland gorillas roam the largest ranges, up to 9 square miles (23 km²). Mountain gorillas find enough food in a range of 1.5 to 3 square miles (4 to 8 km²). The lead silverback keeps a close eye on his group. No one is allowed to wander more than 100 feet (30 m) away. When he beds

Fast Fact!

Gorillas eat up to 40 pounds (18 kg) of food in one day.

down in his circular nest of leafy branches, the others bed down, as well. The silverback also guards against intruders and fathers the group's babies.[6]

A female gorilla gives birth to her first offspring at around age ten. The tiny 4.5-pound (2-kg) newborn clings to its mother's chest when she moves from place to place. As it gains size and strength, the baby shifts to a piggyback position. After nursing for six months or

A young gorilla hitches a piggyback ride from its mother.

so, it begins to sample shoots, leaves, and fruit. At three, the female weans her growing youngster. Like kids everywhere, juveniles love to wrestle, climb trees, and perform wild stunts. Unlike the agile youngsters, the massive adults climb trees only when they must.

Because ranges often overlap, groups sometimes meet at a feeding spot. That is a signal for the two silverback leaders to confront each other. Each male emits a series of low-pitched hoo-hoo-hoo noises that build in volume. Then the silverbacks beat their chests and pound the ground. As the awesome display builds, one of them may make short, sideways charges. To dramatize this show of strength, he rips off branches and tosses them in the air. After long, tense minutes, one of the silverbacks backs down. His group tags along as he knuckle walks into the forest.

Once in a while a silverback will try to steal a rival's females. When that happens, the hooting and chest-beating ends with an earthshaking charge. The combatants grapple while ripping and tearing with their long, sharp canine teeth. Sometimes, the battle ends when the victor inflicts a severe injury on his foe. The loser limps away, bleeding from his wounds. If the gashes become infected, he is likely to die.[7]

These titanic struggles ensure that only the fittest silverbacks father the next generation. Not even King Kong himself, however, could fight off the forces that are pushing gorillas ever closer to extinction.

chapter three

GORILLA THREATS

In July 2007, a silverback mountain gorilla and three females were killed by poachers in the Virunga National Park. A few years earlier, two mountain gorillas were killed and their baby was stolen.

These reports speak to a troubling paradox. In the jungles of Africa, the gorilla's only natural foe is an occasional leopard. Gorillas are endangered because the species that is trying to save them is also their greatest threat. Humans destroy habitat, kill gorillas for profit, and may even spread disease.

Deadly Childhood Disease

Gorillas and humans share a common genetic heritage. That fact complicates the task of saving the gorilla. A childhood disease, such as measles, causes little worry in an American home. Set loose in the jungle, that same virus can be a death sentence. In 1989, one of Rwanda's mountain gorillas died after contracting measles. Fearing the further spread of the disease, veterinarians launched a vaccination program. To their relief, no further cases have been reported among the local gorillas.[1]

Gorillas are prey to much more than measles. Skin disorders and intestinal parasites weaken their victims but seldom kill. Diseases of the throat and lungs take a heavier toll. Many captive gorillas, for example, died in the great flu epidemic of 1918. Today, settlements are pushing higher into mountain gorilla habitat. The gorillas are even contracting diseases such as scabies and polio from humans. As the jungle is cleared away for farming and lumber, gorilla groups must sleep at higher altitudes. Coughs and sniffles can turn into pneumonia when winter nights bring freezing rains.[2]

Karisoke, Dian Fossey's old camp in Rwanda, encourages tourism. To protect both gorillas and visitors, guides enforce a strict set of rules. Anyone who shows symptoms of illness must remain in camp, along with children under the age of fifteen. Out in the jungle, no one is allowed close contact with the mountain gorillas. If a curious youngster approaches, the tourists are told to back up. During the hour visit, those who sneeze or cough must turn their faces away. If visitors break one of the rules, they are sent back to camp. Since these strict rules were adopted, no Karisoke gorilla has come down with a human disease.[3]

Vanishing Forest Homes

The process has been going on for years beyond count; African farmers venture into the forest and clear a plot of land. They plant rows of banana trees and care for them as they grow. The crop is almost ready to pick when disaster strikes. Gorillas slip into the grove in the early morning. They ignore the fruit and feast on the tender inner flesh of the trunks. When the farmers arrive, they find that a year's work has been ruined. To take revenge, they track and kill as many gorillas as they can find. That night the village feasts on gorilla meat.[4]

Why did the farmers need those new fields? The reason can be found in any almanac. Africa's population is more than one billion and growing.[5] Food, homes, and jobs must be found for millions of hungry mouths. That means more farming, more logging, more mining—more of everything. As cities, towns, and villages expand, wildlife habitat vanishes. Civil wars and tribal conflicts add to the problem. Poorly supplied militia soldiers often live off the land. When they are hungry, they turn their rifles on gorillas and other wildlife.

African countries in need of cash open their borders to logging and mining. To reach groups of hardwood trees, loggers cut roads deep into the jungle. If they practice clear cutting, the lush rainforest gives way to a desert landscape. The roads also isolate gorilla groups. When this happens, young gorillas cannot move from group to group. The result is inbreeding and an increase in infant deaths.

Men measure trees destined for export in the Democratic Republic of the Congo.

As the trees fall, villagers follow with their herds and plows. Many practice slash-and-burn farming. After cutting and setting fire to the brush, they plant their crops. In a few years, the soil loses its fertility, forcing the farmers to move on to a new patch of forest. As the cycle repeats itself, the gorilla's food supply dwindles.[6] In Uganda, the Bwindi National Park has lost 60 percent of its gorilla habitat in this way.[7]

The Problem of Poachers

In 1978, Dian Fossey was deeply depressed. Digit, one of the first gorillas to accept her when she began her studies, had been killed. She summed up her findings in these words: "It now appears that many of the Virunga gorillas have recently been killed off by poachers. . . . This could be the beginning of the end of the remaining two hundred or so mountain gorillas."[8]

Farmers in central Africa clear fields using slash-and-burn techniques.

Along with their guns and nets, poachers set hundreds of wire snares. A silverback that catches a hand or a foot in one of these traps often panics. As he thrashes about, the wire cuts him deeper. If the gorilla cannot free himself, he will be easy game for the poachers. If he does break free, his hand or foot may be lost to infection, which can kill the gorilla. The problem is all too common, Mike Nichols discovered. Of eleven gorillas in one group, he noted, "Two have only one hand and a third [has] a deformed hand—the result of early encounters with snares."[9]

Fast Fact!

Young male gorillas leave their troop when they are about eleven years old. They will have their own family group by the time they are fifteen.

Killing gorillas is illegal no matter where the great apes live. Sadly, despite the laws, poachers still sometimes invade the jungles to slaughter the great apes. Some poachers kill the mothers in order to capture babies to sell to zoos or collectors. Others kill the gorilla, butcher it, and sell the bushmeat.

Poachers take tons of bushmeat from the Congo River Basin each year. The total includes pigs, antelopes, and porcupines, as well as chimps and sometimes gorillas. In 2009, undercover work revealed that every week, about two western lowland gorillas were killed in a region of the Congo and sold in the markets as bushmeat.[10]

chapter four
SAVING GORILLAS

Conservationist George Schaller is a recognized biologist at the Wildlife Conservation Society, which is based at the Bronx Zoo in New York. He has traveled to Africa to study the great apes up close. While he learned to love gorillas during the early 1960s, he also worried about their future. There were many dangers: loss of habitat, disease, poaching, civil wars, and the bushmeat trade. He knew these threats were a recipe for extinction. Schaller voiced his concerns with these words:

> Sadly, the most important fact we have learned about gorillas in recent years is that if humankind wishes to share this planet with the apes in centuries to come we can never ignore their existence, falter in vigilance, or fail in total commitment. We must cherish and protect the gorillas forevermore.[1]

Today's naturalists add a footnote to Schaller's plea. Gorillas, they remind us, are a vital part of Africa's ecology. The daily act of eating many kinds of plants helps keep the rainforest healthy. The seed-laden dung dropped by gorillas sprouts useful plants wherever they wander. Even so, gorillas remain on the endangered list. The war to save them dates back almost one hundred years.

Carl Akeley and Dian Fossey

Early explorers shot gorillas on sight. Some pulled the trigger because they feared an attack. Others wanted trophies for themselves or to be displayed in museums. In the 1920s, naturalist Carl Akeley visited the Virunga Volcanoes to collect specimens. The payoff was a display of mountain gorillas that still attracts visitors to the American Museum of Natural History. After that bloody start, Akeley turned into a gorilla protector. He became a prime mover behind the creation of Albert National Park. Today, the old preserve is divided into three national parks. One belongs to Rwanda, one to Uganda, and one to the Congo. Akeley died of malaria in 1926 and was buried in a Virunga meadow.[2]

Dian Fossey began by studying mountain gorillas in the Virungas. She ended up as their friend and guardian. As Fossey warmed to her task, she took great lengths to protect "her" gorillas. She cut traplines. She herded gorillas away from areas where poachers set their snares. After a poacher shot Digit, her much-loved silverback, she set up the Digit Fund. The money raised by the fund helped pay for antipoaching patrols.[3] In 1984 alone, the patrols destroyed more than two thousand snares. A decade later, that number was down to 941 snares. But a civil war in Rwanda had also started and led to an increase in illegal activity. Somehow, the gorillas survived these years during the civil war in good condition even though there were more snares set by poachers.

Fossey used any method that promised to get the job done. What would she do about some herdsmen who were grazing cattle in the park? She put on a Halloween mask, hid in the bushes, and jumped out as the herdsmen passed by. The Africans took one look at what appeared to be a screaming, arm-waving ghost and promptly fled. Fossey next led a raiding party that burned down a poacher's hut. Later, as her patience wore thin, she shot a cow and held dozens more for ransom.[4]

Governments Join the Fight

Thanks to Schaller, Akeley, and Fossey, the public became aware of the gorilla's plight. From schoolkids to film stars, people pitched in to do what they could. Only governments, however, can back up those efforts with big bucks and tough laws. In the United States, one key step was passage of the Endangered Species Act. The act forbids the killing, capture, or sale of any animal or plant listed as endangered. The act also commits the United States to the Convention on International Trade in Endangered Species, or

Dian Fossey's passion was to protect the mountain gorilla.

CITES. This agreement, signed by more than 120 countries, puts strict controls on the sale of endangered plants and animals. A nation that breaks the rules can be cut off from markets and denied loans.

Other laws focus on wild primates and their habitats. The US Congress pledged that it would provide $5 million a year to the cause when it passed the Great Apes Conservation Act of 2000. A similar United Nations program is known as the Great Apes Survival Project, or GRASP. One of the program's aims is to convince African nations they should set aside more game reserves. Several parks have opened, but many western lowland gorillas live in unprotected jungles. GRASP also improves law enforcement by making sure park rangers have modern equipment.

Citing public health fears, governments are joining the campaign against bushmeat. China, for example, has banned the sale of ape meat from Gabon. The problem is greater in Africa, where endangered species laws are often ignored. In Kenya, health officers blame bushmeat for outbreaks of Ebola, meningitis, and anthrax. "Stay healthy!" they warn Kenyans. "Do not eat bushmeat."[5]

Private Help

Governments seldom move quickly. This inspires fears that gorillas will be gone before politicians take action. Nimble nongovernmental organizations, or NGOs, often step in to fill the gap. One of the best-known NGOs is the World Wildlife Fund (WWF). The WWF works to save endangered species, such as koalas, tigers, pandas, and gorillas. Its gorilla programs range from safeguarding habitats to cutting off the trade in gorilla parts and products. A second NGO, Conservation International (CI), was greatly aided by a $261 million gift from Intel founder Gordon Moore. CI plans to use the money to halt extinctions in New Guinea, the Amazon, and the Congo River Basin.

An anti-poaching team from the World Wildlife Fund examines a miner's rifle in a national park in Gabon. Stopping poachers is one of the many ways the WWF works to save endangered species.

Deep in African jungles, other NGOs focus on saving gorillas. Two active groups are the Mountain Gorilla Conservation Fund (MGCF) and the International Gorilla Conservation Program. The Dian Fossey Gorilla Fund International carries on the work of its founder. The fund's goals are gorilla protection, field research, education, and economic development.

Tourists in Uganda are on the lookout for gorillas.

The Mountain Gorilla Conservation Fund tries to enlist governments as allies. In Rwanda, one goal is to promote the gorilla as a national symbol. They support mountain gorillas appearing on Rwandan coins, stamps, and maybe someday the national flag. Locally, the MGCF asks investors to build hotels close to gorilla country. This would give tourists a place to stay and see the gorillas. Tourists mean more jobs and income for the region. If gorillas are to have a future, villagers must see them as valued neighbors.

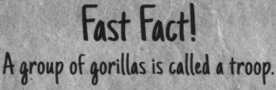

Fast Fact!
A group of gorillas is called a troop.

chapter five

FUTURE OUTLOOK FOR GORILLAS

Take a close look at a mighty silverback gorilla. It is easy to see why these animals are classified as one of our closest relatives. Since their decline in the wild, we have been caring for this special species with captive breeding programs in zoos and stricter conservation plans to help the wild population. Perhaps it is our connection to their complex chain of life over the past millions of years that pulls us to protect them.

Author Dale Peterson explains, "In their faces, bodies, and gestures we see the reflection . . . of our own. Thus we find them beautiful and fascinating, or peculiar and comical. . . . They feel pain, care for their young, care for each other. They are some of the . . . most complex and intelligent of the forest dwellers."[1]

If that is true, why would anyone lop off a branch of our family tree? Out in the jungle, it seems, choices seldom are clear-cut. In 1997, Gary Strieker chanced upon a pitiful baby gorilla in central Africa. The baby's mother had been shot the week before. When the hunter offered to sell the sickly little orphan, Strieker was faced with a tough call. If he bought the baby, he could take it to a rescue

In the Democratic Republic of the Congo, a ranger watches over a gorilla troop.

center in Cameroon. Still, this was Africa. Doing so, he thought, might do more harm than good.

"I'm now a realist," Strieker writes, "accepting that most of the wild animals in the forest along the roads we've traveled will probably disappear in the next decade. Accepting that, I could not buy that baby gorilla. To do so would have encouraged the hunter to go out and capture another—and this one was already too traumatized to survive much longer. I'm a realist—but I still wonder if I did the right thing."[2]

Zoos to the Rescue

Zoos in western Europe and North America have come a long way from the days when they kept animals in small barren cages. Bored and restless, some gorillas ate too much. Others scratched bare spots in their fur or banged their heads against the cage bars. Today's visitors see healthy gorilla groups living in airy, leafy enclosures. The families feed, play, and raise their young much as they would in the wild. Behind the scenes, experts carry on breeding programs designed to maintain a healthy gorilla population. To manage this effort, many zoos belong to a Species Survival Plan. As part of the plan to prevent inbreeding, Chicago's Lincoln Park Zoo trades silverbacks with other zoos. Since 1970, the zoo's females have produced more than fifty babies.[3]

Some critics watch these programs and wonder if the gene pool is too small. Far too many young gorillas, they note, have been sired by a handful of males. Veterinarians treat and save animals that would have died in the wild. Perhaps these gorillas will one

This baby gorilla was born in a zoo in Germany.

day be better adapted to life in zoos than to life in the jungle. How would the great-grandchildren of a once-wild silverback react if set free in the jungle? Writer Bettyann Kevles suggests, only half in jest, that the newly freed gorillas would take one look around, then they would hop the next plane back to the zoo.[4]

Steps for a Bright Future

Keeping zoo-bred animals alive will be a hollow victory if wild gorillas become extinct. If *Gorilla gorilla* is to survive in its natural habitat, naturalists must focus their efforts on central Africa. A three-step plan was promoted in the 1980s. Each step attacks a major threat to the gorilla's survival.

Step 1: Crack down on poachers. If poachers continue to kill gorillas, nothing else will matter. Killing even one group leader can result in an avalanche of deaths. When a new silverback takes over, instinct drives him to sire his own babies. A female, however, cannot become pregnant during the three years she nurses her young. The silverback's response is to kill the female's infant.[5] The answer is to beef up park protection patrols. In 1980, for example, the guard force in Rwanda's Volcanoes Park grew from fourteen men to more than forty. Morale was high. Better paid and equipped with new tents, boots, and rain gear, the guards expanded their patrols. The changes paid off that first year. After the blood bath of 1979, only one park gorilla died from a poacher's bullet the following year.[6]

Step 2: Teach people to value gorillas. All too often, the people who live close to gorilla habitats know little about their wild neighbors. In one study, 25 percent of local farmers could not even describe a gorilla.[7] The team of Bill Weber and Amy Vedder found that Rwanda's school texts contained only two mentions of gorillas. The first described their teeth. The second wrongly stated

Rwandan schoolchildren are taught to value the mountian gorilla.

that they often raided farmer's crops. Weber and Vedder went right to the top. Before they were through, the government had added a conservation unit to the course of study.

Weber then went on tour. He showed high schoolers a film about gorillas and talked about their value. The students glowed with pride when they heard his message. Their country could do something mighty America could not. Rwanda could save the mountain gorilla! Weber's team also carried the message to students and their parents in the Virungas. In addition to lessons about gorillas, farmers learned that their water supply depended on healthy mountain forests. The meaning was clear. If they saved the gorilla and its habitat, they would be saving their crops, as well.[8]

Step 3: Develop ecotourism. Poachers who shoot gorillas with rifles collect a one-time profit. Villages that provide housing, food, and guides to tourists who shoot wildlife with cameras reap a yearly cash harvest. This fact has helped build an ecology-friendly tourist business in the Virungas and the Impenetrable Forest in Uganda. Guides escort small troops of ecotourists into areas where mountain gorillas feed. Over time, these much-visited groups have lost their fear of strangers. During an hour's visit, the tourists creep to within a few yards of the gorillas with cameras clicking. Even though critics charge that these visits make the park less wild and free, the people of Rwanda welcome ecotourism. Before civil war swept the country in 1994, tourism trailed only tea and coffee as a source of national income.[9]

Some scientists, though, are afraid that ecotourism could harm gorillas. When they lose their fear of humans, gorillas may become easier to hunt. In addition, humans might transmit diseases to gorillas.

Former poachers perform for tourists in northern Rwanda. Ex-poachers have formed an association that helps them find new sources of income so they do not have to resort to illegal hunting.

What's Ahead?

The struggle to save the gorilla is more than a fight to preserve one species. Doctors remind us that more than 25 percent of all useful drugs come from rainforest plants. Research labs, however, have tested less than 7 percent of those plants for medical uses. If loggers, poachers, and farmers destroy the rain forests, the cure for diseases, such as AIDS, could be lost, as well.

Let think about the words of our friend Koko. People have long argued that human beings are the only species that can foresee its own death. Maureen Sheehan, one of Koko's trainers, begs to differ. Check out this sign language exchange:

> *Sheehan:* Where do gorillas go when they die?
> *Koko:* Comfortable hole bye.
> *Sheehan:* When do gorillas die?
> *Koko:* Trouble old.[10]

Wise old Koko, it seems, is fully aware of herself and the world around her. No one, of course, expects her to grasp the more complex concept of extinction. In the end, it is up to us to make sure that all great apes have a future. Luckily, some people have had a change of heart. Men who used to be poachers are now working as gamekeepers in Africa. They have followed the urging of conservationists to put down their weapons. They now guard the animals they used to hunt. Money from tourism provides the incentive these men need to protect the gorillas. With continued education, the story of the mountain gorilla may have a happy ending.

Chapter Notes

Chapter 1. Meet *Gorilla gorilla*

1. Dale Peterson, *The Deluge and the Ark: a Journey Into Primate Worlds* (Boston, Mass.: Houghton Mifflin Company, 1989), p. 111.

2. Dr. Angela Meder, "Gorillas in African Culture and Medicine," *Gorilla Journal,* June 18, 1999, <http://www.berggorilla.org/en/gorillas/people-gorillas/human-gorilla-article-view/artikel/gorillas-in-african-culture-and-medicine/> (January 28, 2015).

3. "King Kong," (1933), *Greatest Films,* n.d., <http://www.filmsite.org/kingk.html> (January 28, 2015).

4. Peterson, p. 112.

5. Sarel Eimerl and Irven DeVore, *The Primates* (New York, N.Y.: Time-Life Books, 1974), p. 64.

6. Peterson, pp. 112–113.

7. Michael Nichols, *The Great Apes: Between Two Worlds* (Washington, D.C.: National Geographic Society, 1993), p. 37.

8. Peterson, p. 331.

Chapter 2. Jungle Gorilla

1. Bettyann Kevles, *Thinking Gorillas: Testing and Teaching the Greatest Ape* (New York, N.Y.: E. P. Dutton, 1980), p. 32.

2. Ibid., p. 6.

3. Michael Kavanagh, *A Complete Guide to Monkeys, Apes and Other Primates* (New York, N.Y.: Viking Press, 1983), pp. 18–19.

4. Dale Peterson, *The Deluge and the Ark: a Journey Into Primate Worlds* (Boston, Mass.: Houghton Mifflin Company, 1989), pp. 108–109.

5. Noel Rowe, *The Pictorial Guide to the Living Primates* (East Hampton, N.Y.: Pogonias Press, 1996), pp. 224–227.

6. Sy Montgomery, *Walking with the Great Apes: Jane Goodall, Dian Fossey, Biruté Galdikas* (Boston, Mass.: Houghton Mifflin, 1991), p. 50.

7. Boyd Norton, *The Mountain Gorilla* (Stillwater, Minn.: Voyageur Press, 1990), pp. 65, 68.

Chapter 3. Gorilla Threats

1. Martha M. Robbins, Pascale Sicotte, and Kelly J. Stewart, eds., *Mountain Gorillas: Three Decades of Research at Karisoke* (Cambridge, UK: Cambridge University Press, 2001), p. 301.

2. Bettyann Kevles, *Thinking Gorillas: Testing and Teaching the Greatest Ape* (New York, N.Y.: E. P. Dutton, 1980), p. 31.

3. Robbins, pp. 353–354.

4. Michael Nichols, George B. Schaller, and Nan Richardson, ed., *Gorilla: Struggle for Survival in the Virungas* (New York, N.Y.: Aperture Foundation, 1989), p. 10.

5. World Population Statistics, Africa Population 2013, May 20, 2013, <http://www.worldpopulationstatistics.com/africa-population-2013> (January 28, 2015).

6. Dale Peterson, *The Deluge and the Ark: A Journey Into Primate Worlds* (Boston, Mass.: Houghton Mifflin Company, 1989), pp. 89–90.

7. Anthony L. Rose, "Wildlife Protectors Fund—African Journal," *Gorilla, Journal of the Gorilla Foundation,* Spring 2002, p. 13.

8. Farley Mowat, *Woman in the Mists: the Story of Dian Fossey and the Mountain Gorillas of Africa* (New York, N.Y.: Warner Books, 1987), p. 165.

9. Nichols, pp. 20–21.

10. "Gorillas Hunted for Bushmeat in Congo," *Smithsonian.com,* September 16, 2009, < http://www.smithsonianmag.com/science-nature/gorillas-hunted-for-bushmeat-in-congo-17014330/?no-ist > (January 28, 2015).

Chapter 4. Saving Gorillas

1. Quoted in Boyd Norton, *The Mountain Gorilla* (Stillwater, Minn.: Voyageur Press, 1990), p. 23.

2. Bill Weber and Amy Vedder, *In the Kingdom of Gorillas: Fragile Species in a Dangerous Land* (New York, N.Y.: Simon & Schuster, 2001), pp. 42–43.

3. Martha M. Robbins, Pascale Sicotte, and Kelly J. Stewart, eds., *Mountain Gorillas: Three Decades of Research at Karisoke* (Cambridge, UK: Cambridge University Press, 2001), p. 365.

4. Weber, p. 239.

5. Sara Root, "African Gorilla Update," *Gorilla, Journal of the Gorilla Foundation,* Spring 2002, p. 13.

Chapter 5. Future Outlook for Gorillas

1. Dale Peterson, *The Deluge and the Ark: A Journey Into Primate Worlds* (Boston, Mass.: Houghton Mifflin Company, 1989), p. 334.

2. Gary Strieker, "Ethical Dilemmas in the Wild," *CNN Wild Planet Notebook,* (April 1, 1997), < http://www.cnn.com/EARTH/9704/01/wild.planet.notebook/index.html> (January 28, 2015).

3. Lincoln Park Zoo. Posts from the President. "Welcoming a Gorilla Baby," October 16, 2012, <http://www.lpzoo.org/blog/posts-president/welcoming-gorilla-baby> (January 28, 2015).

4. Bettyann Kevles, *Thinking Gorillas: Testing and Teaching the Greatest Ape* (New York, N.Y.: E. P. Dutton, 1980), pp. 153–154.

5. Bill Weber and Amy Vedder, *In the Kingdom of Gorillas: Fragile Species in a Dangerous Land* (New York, N.Y.: Simon & Schuster, 2001), p. 87.

6. Ibid., pp. 216–217.

7. "Conservation Issues," *Gorillas,* 1999, < http://seaworld.org/en/animal-info/animal-infobooks/gorilla/conservation-and-research> (January 28, 2015).

8. Weber, pp. 133, 204–205.

9. Peterson, p. 128.

10. Peterson, p. 333.

GLOSSARY

breeding program—A plan used to reproduce animals for a few generations. Often used by conservationists to reproduce species that are endangered.

bushmeat—Meat from wild animals, such as chimpanzees and gorillas.

captive—Being confined or held in a safe place.

conservation—The protection of plants, animals, and natural resources.

ecotourism—Traveling to a natural place to learn about the habitat and culture without damaging the environment.

endangered—In danger of becoming extinct and not existing on earth anymore.

extinction—The death of an entire group, or species, of living things.

great apes—Gorillas, chimpanzees, bonobos (pygmy chimps), and orangutans.

pneumonia—A disease of the lungs. It can be caused by bacteria or viruses.

poacher—A person who kills or steals wild animals illegally.

population—The total number of people, animals, or plants living in a specific area.

primate—A member of a group of animals that includes humans, apes, and monkeys.

silverback—An older male gorilla with white or gray hair on its back. The silverback is usually a dominant gorilla.

species—A group of animals or plants that have similar features. They can produce offspring of the same kind.

threatened—A group of animals that is close to becoming endangered.

FURTHER READING

Books

Claus, Matteson. *Animals and Deforestation*. New York, N.Y.: Gareth Stevens Publishing, 2014.

Doak, Robin S. *Dian Fossey: Friend to Africa's Gorillas*. Brookvale, Australia: Raintree, 2014.

Hirsch, Rebecca. *Mountain Gorillas: Powerful Forest Mammals*. Minneapolis, Minn.: Lerner Publishing Group, 2015.

Miller-Schroeder, Patricia. *Gorillas*. New York, N.Y.: Weigl Publishers, Inc., 2012.

Lewin, Betsy. *Gorilla Walk*. New York, N.Y.: Lee & Low Books, 2014.

Yolen, Jane. *Animal Stories: Heartwarming True Tales from the Animal Kingdom*. Washington, D.C.: National Geographic Children's Books, 2014.

Web Sites

endangeredspeciesinternational.org/gorillas.html

Facts about gorilla species, habitat, threats, and conservation.

gorillafund.org

Read about the work being done by The Dian Fossey Gorilla Fund.

saveagorilla.org

Learn more about the Mountain Gorilla Education Fund.

INDEX